FAITH'S LITTLE INSTRUCTION BOOK FOR HEALING

Supercharged Quotes To Blast Sickness Out of Your Life!

Harrison House, Inc.
Tulsa, Oklahoma

Unless otherwise indicated, all Scripture quotations are taken from the *King James Version* of the Bible.

"Prayer for Healing" is based on "Healing" from *Prayers That Avail Much for Teens,* copyright © 1991, 1994 by Word Ministries, Inc. Published by Harrison House, Inc., Tulsa, Oklahoma.

Introduction

Faith's Little Instruction Book for Healing is a unique collection of powerful, faith-building quotes on healing from leading Spirit-filled men and women of past and present. These quotes, coupled with Scriptures, will strengthen and encourage you to stand firm and trust in the promises of God for your healing.

Based upon the best selling books, *Faith's Little Instruction Book I* and *Faith's Little Instruction Book II*, this little book will challenge you to do more than stand by and allow the enemy to rob you of your health. You will be moved into action to put God's Word into practice as you walk in divine health through faith. These quotes will stir your spirit as you read from

Kenneth E. Hagin, Kenneth Copeland, Gloria Copeland, T.L. Osborn, F.F. Bosworth, E.W. Kenyon, Creflo Dollar, Jr., Frederick K.C. Price and many others.

This book is a treasury of wisdom on healing from some of the greatest people of faith in our times, but more importantly, it is a treasury of the timeless wisdom and guidance of the Bible. *Faith's Little Instruction Book for Healing* was designed to be a burst of hope and inspiration -- we pray that it is in your life!

The world does not need our creeds or denominational lingo. It's time we got back to preaching the old-fashioned, heartfelt, Holy Ghost, sin-eradicating, life-changing, body-healing gospel of Jesus Christ.

Rod Parsley

And Jesus went about all the cities and villages, teaching in their synagogues, and preaching the gospel of the kingdom, and healing every sickness and every disease among the people.

Matthew 9:35

God's Medicine: To be spoken by mouth three times a day until faith comes, then once a day to maintain faith. If circumstances grow worse, double the dosage. There are no harmful side effects.

Charles Capps

Let us hold fast the profession of our faith without wavering; (for he is faithful that promised).

Hebrews 10:23

Until the person seeking healing is sure from God's Word that it is God's will to heal him, he is trying to reap a harvest where there is no seed planted.

F.F. Bosworth

So then faith cometh by hearing, and hearing by the word of God.

Romans 10:17

The road to divine healing is seldom an expressway.

Kenneth E. Hagin

Because strait is the gate, and narrow is the way, which leadeth unto life, and few there be that find it.

Matthew 7:14

8

To receive healing is wonderful, but to live in divine health is better.

Gloria Copeland

Grace and peace be multiplied to you by the knowledge of our Lord. Inasmuch as his power divine has bestowed upon us every requisite for life and godliness by the knowledge of him who called us to his own glory and excellence.

2 Peter 1:2,3 Moffatt

9

You must *know* that you *know* that you *know* healing is yours down in your own "*knower*"!!

Billy Joe Daugherty

When any one hears the word of the kingdom, and does not understand it, the evil one comes and snatches away what has been sown in his heart....

Matthew 13:19 NAS

10

There is no sickness problem. There is simply a problem of the believer's coming to know his inheritance in Christ.

E.W. Kenyon

Christ hath redeemed us from the curse of the law, being made a curse for us: for it is written, Cursed is every one that hangeth on a tree: That the blessing of Abraham might come on the Gentiles through Jesus Christ; that we might receive the promise of the Spirit through faith.

Galatians 3:13,14

Some people wonder why they can't have faith for healing. They feed their body three hot meals a day and their spirit one cold snack a week.

F.F. Bosworth

...Desire the sincere milk of the word, that ye may grow thereby.

1 Peter 2:2

[Jesus has] given us all authority and power to stomp on sin and sickness and every demonic thing in the earth! Put the works of Satan under your feet....

Kenneth Copeland

And hath put all things under his [Jesus'] feet, and gave him to be the head over all things to the church, which is his body, the fulness of him that filleth all in all.

Ephesians 1:22,23

13

How glorious to be able to tell each sick one, no matter what the disease from which they are suffering, that Christ has redeemed them from it....

Lilian B. Yeomans, M.D.

Who hath delivered us from the power of darkness, and hath translated us into the kingdom of his dear Son: In whom we have redemption through his blood....

Colossians 1:13,14

Expectancy is the atmosphere for miracles.

Edwin Louis Cole

And God did unusual and extraordinary miracles by the hands of Paul, so that handkerchiefs or towels or aprons which had touched his skin were carried away and put upon the sick, and their diseases left them....

Acts 19:11,12 AMP

Faith looks beyond the walls of the obstacle and to the answer.

Benny Hinn

They went up on the roof and lowered him [the paralytic] on his mat through the tiles into the middle of the crowd, right in front of Jesus. When Jesus saw their faith, he said, "Friend, your sins are forgiven."

Luke 5:19,20 NIV

No matter what a man's privileges are, if the hand of faith is paralyzed he cannot take hold of them.

E.W. Kenyon

Now do not drop that confidence of yours; it carries with it a rich hope of reward. Steady patience is what you need, so that after doing the will of God you may receive what you were promised.

Hebrews 10:35,36 Moffatt

17

Only a pure, hungry, seeking heart will ever recline on the furnishings of healing.

Ed Dufresne

But without faith it is impossible to please him: for he that cometh to God must believe that he is, and that he is a rewarder of them that diligently seek him.

Hebrews 11:6

God is still forgiving sins, and He is still healing diseases, or else He is not the same God He used to be.

Dr. T.J. McCrossan

Bless the Eternal, O my soul, remember all his benefits; he pardons all your sins, and all your sicknesses he heals.

Psalm 103:2,3
Moffatt

There is no such thing as the Lord not meeting your need. There are no "if's" or "may's"; His promises are all "shall's."

Smith Wigglesworth

But my God shall supply all your need according to his riches in glory by Christ Jesus.

Philippians 4:19

Many do not believe it is opposing God's will to be kept alive as long as possible by medicine, machines, and every other means, but they believe that *praying* to stay alive is working against God!

Kenneth E. Hagin

. . . the prayer of the upright is his delight.

Proverbs 15:8

21

Calvary was a double cure. Number one, it saved us from an eternity spent in hell. Number two, it healed our physical body. That is the gospel of Jesus Christ.

Rod Parsley

He personally bore our sins in His [own] body on the tree [as on an altar and offered Himself on it], that we might die (cease to exist) to sin and live to righteousness. By His wounds you have been healed.

1 Peter 2:24 AMP

God doesn't care whether you go to the physician or the minister to get healing as long as you put His Word first place in your life.

Jerry Savelle

He sent his word, and healed them, and delivered them from their destructions.

Psalm 107:20

23

When you come into the family of God, when you get to the place where Jesus is Lord of your life, there are certain rights and privileges that you will have simply by being "on the team," by being in the family of God.

Buddy Harrison

No weapon that is formed against thee shall prosper; and every tongue that shall rise against thee in judgment thou shalt condemn. This is the heritage of the servants of the Lord, and their righteousness is of me, saith the Lord.

Isaiah 54:17

If ye WERE [healed], ye ARE, if ye ARE, ye "IS."

Frederick K.C. Price

Who his own self bare our sins in his own body on the tree, that we, being dead to sins, should live unto righteousness: by whose stripes ye were healed.

1 Peter 2:24

The time will come
that you will need faith,
either for yourself,
or some member of
your family. And if you
haven't kept your faith
strong, you'll be at
a disadvantage.

P.C. Nelson

Finally, my brethren, be strong in the Lord, and in the power of his might. Put on the whole armour of God, that ye may be able to stand against the wiles of the devil.

Ephesians 6:10,11

God has handed you the reins of the universe and said, "Drive on victoriously through this life to the City of God." That's *dominion*!

Lester Sumrall

"I will give you the keys of the kingdom of heaven; and whatever you shall bind on earth shall be bound in heaven, and whatever you shall loose on earth shall be loosed in heaven."

Matthew 16:19 NAS

27

God is looking for men and women who will stand on His Word believing that if He said it, He will do it, and that if He spoke it, He will bring it to pass.

R.W. Schambach

...You know in all your hearts and in all your souls that not one word of all the good words which the Lord your God spoke concerning you has failed; all have been fulfilled for you, not one of them has failed.

Joshua 23:14 NAS

Understanding the compassion which God has toward you will totally change your attitude about spending time in His presence...it is only in His presence that you can enjoy the benefits of healing, prosperity, peace and power.

Creflo Dollar, Jr.

One thing have I desired of the LORD, that will I seek after; that I may dwell in the house of the LORD all the days of my life, to behold the beauty of the LORD, and to enquire in his temple. For in the time of trouble he shall hide me in his pavilion: in the secret of his tabernacle shall he hide me; he shall set me up upon a rock.
Psalm 27:4,5

Your symptoms may point you to death, but God's Word points you to life, and you cannot look in these opposite directions at the same time.

F.F. Bosworth

See, I have set before you today life and prosperity, and death and adversity ... So choose life in order that you may live, you and your descendants....

Deuteronomy 30:15,19 NAS

If Jesus bore our sicknesses and carried our pains, there is no need for both of us to bear them!

Kenneth E. Hagin

And yet ours was the pain he bore, the sorrow he endured! We thought him suffering from a stroke at God's own hand; yet he was wounded because we had sinned, 'twas our misdeeds that crushed him; 'twas for our welfare that he was chastised, the blows that fell to him have brought us healing.

Isaiah 53:4,5 Moffatt

The Word says you are healed. Get used to acting on the Word.

E.W. Kenyon

He sent his word to heal them and preserve their life.

Psalm 107:20 Moffatt

Keep your foot on the devil's neck by standing on the Word of God, and you will see tremendous results!

Jesse Duplantis

...And this is the victory that overcometh the world, even our faith.

1 John 5:4

33

There are many today who have their confidence in things seen. If they would only get their eyes on God instead of on natural things, how quickly they would be helped.

Smith Wigglesworth

By faith we understand that the worlds were prepared by the word of God, so that what is seen was not made out of things which are visible.

Hebrews 11:3 NAS

If sickness is the will of God, then every physician would be a lawbreaker, every trained nurse a defier of the Almighty, and every hospital a house of rebellion instead of a house of mercy.

T.L. Osborn

Those who are strong have no need of a doctor, but those who are ill. Go and learn the meaning of this word, I care for mercy, not for sacrifice.

Matthew 9:12,13 Moffatt

If it was not God's will to heal you, He shouldn't have.

Rod Parsley

But He was wounded for our transgressions, He was bruised for our guilt and iniquities; the chastisement [needful to obtain] peace and well-being for us was upon Him, and with the stripes [that wounded] Him we are healed and made whole.

Isaiah 53:5 AMP

God's best is for the believer to take His Word that says he is healed, put that Word in his heart, confess it with his lips, and allow it to be medicine to his flesh.

Jerry Savelle

"I tell you truly, whoever says to this hill, 'Take and throw yourself into the sea,' and has not a doubt in his mind but believes that what he says will happen, he will have it done. So I tell you, whatever you pray for and ask, believe you have got it, and you shall have it."

Mark 11:23,24 Moffatt

37

God doesn't go
by what you have
been taught. He goes
according to what
He has given you
in the Bible.

Norvel Hayes

*And my message
and my preaching
were not in
persuasive words of
wisdom, but in
demonstration of
the Spirit and of
power, that your
faith should not rest
on the wisdom
of men, but on
the power of God.*

1 Corinthians 2:4,5
NAS

Healing is a forever-settled subject because *God's Word* is forever settled.

Kenneth Hagin, Jr.

For ever, O LORD, thy word is settled in heaven.

Psalm 119:89

39

The most important thing in receiving God's blessings is not our great faith but *His* great faithfulness.

Joyce Meyer

It is of the LORD'S mercies that we are not consumed, because his compassions fail not. They are new every morning: great is thy faithfulness.

Lamentations 3:22,23

40

Too often an event or occurrence is blamed on the "sovereignty of God," when actually God has delegated the authority to the people involved.

Buddy Harrison

"And these signs will accompany those who have believed: in My name they will cast out demons, they will speak with new tongues; they will pick up serpents, and if they drink any deadly poison, it shall not hurt them; they will lay hands on the sick, and they will recover."

Mark 16:17,18 NAS

41

God's Word does not say that by His stripes you *may* be healed. The Word says, *by His stripes you were healed*.

Kenneth Copeland

...By whose stripes ye were healed.

1 Peter 2:24

Asking for healing while refusing to be led by the Spirit is like asking a carpenter to repair the house while refusing to let him in the house.

F.F. Bosworth

If you live in Me [abide vitally united to Me] and My words remain in you and continue to live in your hearts, ask whatever you will, and it shall be done for you.

John 15:7 AMP

43

It's just plain stupid to doubt God.

Norvel Hayes

God is not a man, that he should lie, nor a son of man, that he should change his mind. Does he speak and then not act? Does he promise and not fulfill?

Numbers 23:19 NIV

44

Miracles have never passed away, some people just quit believing.

Gloria Copeland

The grass withers, the flower fades, but the word of our God stands forever.

Isaiah 40:8 NAS

45

Sickness is an invasion of an outlaw force seeking to rob you of your health.

Billy Joe Daugherty

Be sober, be vigilant; because your adversary the devil, as a roaring lion, walketh about, seeking whom he may devour.

1 Peter 5:8

Everything there is in the redemption of Jesus Christ is available for man when man will present his claim in faith and take it. There is no question in the mind of God concerning the salvation of a sinner. No more is there question concerning the healing of the sick one.

John G. Lake

I tell you truly, whoever says to this hill, "take and throw yourself into the sea," and has not a doubt in his mind but believes that what he says will happen, he will have it done.

Mark 11:23 Moffatt

47

When God's Word concerning healing takes root in your flesh, it becomes greater than disease and healing is the result.

Charles Capps

"It is the Spirit who gives life; the flesh profits nothing; the words that I have spoken to you are spirit and are life."

John 6:63 NAS

48

Did you know that Jesus built you and me a house of healing two thousand years ago? But that house of healing Jesus built for us will remain vacant until we decide to move into it.

Ed Dufresne

Christ redeemed us from the curse of the law by becoming a curse for us, for it is written: "Cursed is everyone who is hung on a tree." He redeemed us in order that the blessing given to Abraham might come to the Gentiles through Christ Jesus, so that by faith we might receive the promise of the Spirit.

Galatians 3:13,14 NIV

49

God wants His people well, but it is up to us to make the decision to walk in health.

Marilyn Hickey

"You shall walk in all the way which the Lord your God has commanded you, that you may live, and that it may be well with you, and that you may prolong your days in the land which you shall possess."

Deuteronomy 5:33
NAS

If Satan can keep you in the *sense realm*, he will destroy you – but if you keep him in the *faith realm*, you'll put him under your feet.

Frederick K.C. Price

Above all, taking the shield of faith, wherewith ye shall be able to quench all the fiery darts of the wicked.

Ephesians 6:16

51

As far as Jesus is concerned, you're not the sick trying to get healed. You're the healed and Satan is trying to steal your health.

Gloria Copeland

The thief comes only in order to steal and kill and destroy. I came that they may have and enjoy life, and have it in abundance (to the full, till it overflows).

John 10:10 AMP

Multitudes of people are only half blessed and half healed because they have not been taught the full truth.

Lester Sumrall

...If ye continue in my word, then are ye my disciples indeed; and ye shall know the truth, and the truth shall make you free.

John 8:31,32

53

God does not need sickness and tragedy to teach you anything. He has His Word and His Holy Spirit to teach you whatever you need to know.

Creflo Dollar, Jr.

But the Comforter, which is the Holy Ghost, whom the Father will send in my name, he shall teach you all things, and bring all things to your remembrance, whatsoever I have said unto you.

John 14:26

It is not what God *can* do, but what we know He *yearns* to do, that inspires faith.

F.F. Bosworth

And a leper came to Him, beseeching Him and falling on his knees before Him, and saying to Him, "If You are willing, You can make me clean." And moved with compassion, He stretched out His hand and touched him, and said to him, "I am willing; be cleansed."

Mark 1:40,41 NAS

You are not going to get God to heal you through cheap faith or lazy faith or nonchalant faith.

Norvel Hayes

But without faith it is impossible to please him: for he that cometh to God must believe that he is, and that he is a rewarder of them that diligently seek him.

Hebrews 11:6

The faith seed of the Word concerning your healing must be planted in you before you can successfully reap the healing harvest.

Gloria Copeland

"And the one on whom seed was sown on the good soil, this is the man who hears the word and understands it; who indeed bears fruit, and brings forth, some a hundredfold, some sixty, and some thirty."

Matthew 13:23 NAS

Remember, being whole involves more than just your own life. God's plan for you also calls for ministry to others.

Billy Joe Daugherty

Then he called his twelve disciples together, and gave them power and authority over all devils, and to cure diseases. And he sent them to preach the kingdom of God, and to heal the sick.

Luke 9:1,2

A sick soul invites a sick body.

Gordon Lindsay

A calm and undisturbed mind and heart are the life and health of the body, but envy, jealousy, and wrath are like rottenness of the bones.

Proverbs 14:30 AMP

God always was the healer. He is the healer still, and will ever remain the healer.

John G. Lake

For I am the LORD, I change not....

Malachi 3:6

Faith moves first; then God moves in answer to faith.

Smith Wigglesworth

"Who touched me?" Jesus asked...Then the woman...fell at his feet.... Then he said to her, "Daughter, your faith has healed you...."

Luke 8:45, 47, 48 NIV

61

Faith heals, sets free, receives from God, and walks in liberty.

Ray McCauley

It is for freedom that Christ has set us free. Stand firm, then, and do not let yourselves be burdened again by a yoke of slavery.

Galatians 5:1 NIV

Disease and sickness are never the will of the Father. To believe that they are, is to be disillusioned by the adversary.

E.W. Kenyon

And the very God of peace sanctify you wholly; and I pray God your whole spirit and soul and body be preserved blameless unto the coming of our Lord Jesus Christ.

1 Thessalonians 5:23

When unbelief kept Christ from healing the sick on earth, it will surely do so today.

Dr. T.J. McCrossan

And he did not many mighty works there because of their unbelief.

Matthew 13:58

Whether it is an instant miracle or a recovery, God still wants to heal!

Marilyn Hickey

Many are the afflictions of the righteous: but the LORD delivereth him out of them all.

Psalm 34:19

If God is the author of sickness and disease, yet God healed people through Jesus, then God would be working against Himself!

Kenneth E. Hagin

And if a kingdom be divided against itself, that kingdom cannot stand. And if a house be divided against itself, that house cannot stand.

Mark 3:24,25

66

Tradition is the thief of power. There is no area of our lives where that theft is more evident than in the area of divine healing.

Rod Parsley

So for the sake of your tradition (the rules handed down by your forefathers), you have set aside the Word of God [depriving it of force and authority and making it of no effect].

Matthew 15:6 AMP

When believed and acted upon, any promise of God is transformed into the power of God.

T.L. Osborn

For I am not ashamed of the gospel of Christ: for it is the power of God unto salvation to every one that believeth....

Romans 1:16

When you learn to be moved by God's Word – not by circumstances, not by how you feel or what you see – you can receive anything that God's Word offers.

Gloria Copeland

Now faith is being sure of what we hope for and certain of what we do not see.

Hebrews 11:1 NIV

We should never try
to figure out God's
timetables. He is
always on time.
It's never too late.

R.W. Schambach

"For my thoughts are not your thoughts, neither are your ways my ways," declares the LORD. "As the rain and the snow come down from heaven, and do not return to it without watering the earth...so is my word that goes out from my mouth: It will not return to me empty, but will accomplish what I desire and achieve the purpose for which I sent it."

Isaiah 55:8,10,11 NIV

Pity may give comfort to your emotions, but it won't get you healed. Compassion, on the other hand, is God's love that dares to speak the truth boldly.

Billy Joe Daugherty

For we have not an high priest which cannot be touched with the feeling of our infirmities...Let us therefore come boldly unto the throne of grace, that we may obtain mercy, and find grace to help in time of need.

Hebrews 4:15,16

If we are comfortably settled in unchallenging company, where there is no real obedience of faith, then we must jump over the side, right over human opinion, and make for Jesus out there in the miracle waters.

Reinhard Bonnke

...Ye should earnestly contend for the faith which was once delivered unto the saints.

Jude 3

73

The Living Word in your lips makes you a victor, makes disease and poverty your servants.

E.W. Kenyon

Wherefore God also hath highly exalted him, and given him a name which is above every name: That at the name of Jesus every knee should bow, of things in heaven, and things in earth, and things under the earth; And that every tongue should confess that Jesus Christ is LORD, to the glory of God the Father.

Philippians 2:9-11

Many people miss healing by trying to confine God to miracles. Christ's promise is that "they shall recover," but He does not say "instantly."

F.F. Bosworth

Fear thou not; for I am with thee: be not dismayed; for I am thy God: I will strengthen thee; yea, I will help thee; yea, I will uphold thee with the right hand of my righteousness.

Isaiah 41:10

People with faith will believe that God will do something for them, even if they have never seen God do it for anyone else!

Ed Dufresne

And behold, a woman who had suffered from a flow of blood for twelve years came up behind Him and touched the fringe of His garment; For she kept saying to herself, If I only touch His garment, I shall be restored to health. Jesus turned around and, seeing her, He said, Take courage, daughter! Your faith has made you well. And at once the woman was restored to health.

Matthew 9:20-22 AMP

At Calvary, there was a great healing transfer where the responsibility for healing was switched from God giving it to you receiving it.

Rod Parsley

78

As sin is the manifestation of spiritual death in the *heart* of man, sickness is the manifestation of spiritual death in the *body* of man.

Gloria Copeland

Therefore, just as through one man sin entered the world, and death through sin, and so death spread to all men, because all sinned.

Romans 5:12 NAS

79

The attention you give to the word of healing is determined by how much you value health in your life and how you value the Word of God.

Billy Joe Daugherty

My son, attend to what I say, bend your ear to my words; never lose sight of them, but fix them in your mind; to those who find them, they are life, and health to all their being.

*Proverbs 4:20-22
Moffatt*

A sick person is a poor soul-winner. A physically afflicted person requires the services of the Church instead of serving it.

Gordon Lindsay

Is any sick among you? let him call for the elders of the church; and let them pray over him, anointing him with oil in the name of the LORD.

James 5:14

81

Hope says, "I will get it sometime." Faith says, "I have it now."

E.W. Kenyon

Now faith is the substance of things hoped for, the evidence of things not seen.

Hebrews 11:1

With God "someday" never comes. Faith is right now.

Norvel Hayes

"Therefore I tell you, whatever you ask for in prayer, believe that you have received it, and it will be yours."

Mark 11:24 NIV

When it comes to the benefits of Christ's redemptive work, all are on an equal basis.

T.L. Osborn

Christ redeemed us from the curse of the Law, having become a curse for us – for it is written, "CURSED IS EVERYONE WHO HANGS ON A TREE" – in order that in Christ Jesus the blessing of Abraham might come to the Gentiles, so that we might receive the promise of the Spirit through faith.

Galatians 3:13,14 NAS

Don't doubt God.
If you must doubt
something, doubt
your doubts, because
they are unreliable;
but never doubt God,
nor His Word.

F.F. Bosworth

God is not a man, that he should lie; neither the son of man, that he should repent: hath he said, and shall he not do it? or hath he spoken, and shall he not make it good?

Numbers 23:19

There is a God-ward side and a man-ward side to every battle and to every blessing. God has His part to play, but man also has his part to play.

Kenneth E. Hagin

The LORD will make you the head, not the tail. If you pay attention to the commands of the LORD your God that I give you this day and carefully follow them, you will always be at the top, never at the bottom.

Deuteronomy 28:13 NIV

Believing in healing is not enough. You must know that it is God's will for *you* to be healed.

Gloria Copeland

When evening came, they brought to Him many who were under the power of demons, and He drove out the spirits with a word and restored to health all who were sick. And thus He fulfilled what was spoken by the prophet Isaiah, He Himself took [in order to carry away] our weaknesses and infirmities and bore away our diseases.

Matthew 8:16,17 AMP

87

Healing is just as
valid in this hour
as forgiveness is
valid in this hour.

Billy Joe Daugherty

*Who his own self
bare our sins in his
own body on the
tree, that we, being
dead to sins, should
live unto righteous-
ness: by whose
stripes ye were
healed.*

1 Peter 2:24

88

If we would have Divine health, it is necessary that we obey the laws of health, even in good causes.

Gordon Lindsay

My son, do not forget my law, but let your heart keep my commands; for length of days and long life and peace they will add to you.

Proverbs 3:1,2 NKJV

As long as we think that disease is purely physical, we will not get our deliverance. But when we know it is spiritual, and it must be healed by the Word of God, for you remember He said, "He sent His Word and healed them," then healing becomes a reality.

E.W. Kenyon

...Speak the word only, and my servant shall be healed.

Matthew 8:8

Is there any reason why you should not have faith in God? Has God ever broken one of His promises? I defy any infidel or unbeliever to place a finger on a single promise of God ever made and failed to fulfill.

D.L. Moody

Blessed be the LORD, Who has given rest to His people Israel, according to all that He promised. Not one word has failed of all His good promise which He promised through Moses His servant.

1 Kings 8:56 AMP

It is impossible for one ever to pray with faith until the "If" has been removed from his prayer.

F.F. Bosworth

The prayer of faith will restore the sick man, and the Lord will raise him up; even the sins he has committed will be forgiven him.

James 5:15 Moffatt

When someone gets healed, the Kingdom of God is revealed, for His Kingdom is a Kingdom of wholeness...of well-being...of life.

Billy Joe Daugherty

The thief cometh not, but for to steal, and to kill, and to destroy: I am come that they might have life, and that they might have it more abundantly.

John 10:10

Some people who are healed instantly forget God. On the other hand, those who get better gradually as they continue to believe God's Word develop strong faith.

Kenneth E. Hagin

And Jesus answering said, Were there not ten cleansed? but where are the nine? There are not found that returned to give glory to God, save this stranger. And he said unto him, Arise, go thy way: thy faith hath made thee whole.

Luke 17:17-19

God's way of doing everything is by making promises and then fulfilling them wherever they produce faith.

F. F. Bosworth

Let us hold fast the confession of our hope without wavering, for He who promised is faithful.

Hebrews 10:23 NAS

Healing is an expression of God's love for us which says that God does not want us to perish in our bodies.

Billy Joe Daugherty

Beloved, I wish above all things that thou mayest prosper and be in health, even as thy soul prospereth.

3 John 2

When you know that "by His stripes you are healed" and you know it as you know that two and two are four, the adversary will have no power over you.

E.W. Kenyon

...For this purpose the Son of God was manifested, that he might destroy the works of the devil.

1 John 3:8

97

Yes, the very same faith which saves the soul heals the body, and this faith is the gift of God....

Dr. T.J. McCrossan

Bless the LORD, O my soul, and forget not all his benefits: Who forgiveth all thine iniquities; who healeth all thy diseases.

Psalm 103:2,3

Healing is primarily a faith proposition on the part of the individual who receives.

Kenneth E. Hagin

Does He then, who provides you with the Spirit and works miracles among you, do it by the works of the Law, or by hearing with faith?

Galatians 3:5 NAS

The message of
healing will give
back to you in the
same way that you
give to it.

Billy Joe Daugherty

*And He said to
them, Be careful
what you are
hearing. The
measure [of thought
and study] you give
[to the truth you
hear] will be the
measure [of virtue
and knowledge] that
comes back to you —
and more [besides]
will be given to
you who hear.*

Mark 4:24 AMP

There has never been a miracle drug that could equal the Word of God. God's medicine is the answer to *every* need.

Gloria Copeland

And my God will meet all your needs according to his glorious riches in Christ Jesus.

Philippians 4:19 NIV

Faith is acting in the face of contrary evidence. The Senses declare, "It cannot be," but Faith shouts above the turmoil, "It is!"

E.W. Kenyon

Now faith is being sure of what we hope for and certain of what we do not see.

Hebrews 11:1 NIV

If you're sick in a hospital, God will take advantage of the situation and show His love through you to the lost that are there. But that isn't His perfect will for you. He'd rather you win the whole hospital to the LORD *while you're well*.

Ed Dufresne

Beloved, I pray you may prosper in every way and keep well....

3 John 2 Moffatt

Faith rests on far more solid ground than the evidence of the senses, and that is the Word of God which "abideth forever."

F.F. Bosworth

We live by faith, not by sight.

2 Corinthians 5:7
NIV

God is glorified
through healing
and deliverance,
not through sickness
and suffering.

Kenneth E. Hagin

*For ye are bought
with a price:
therefore glorify God
in your body and in
your spirit, which
are God's.*

1 Corinthians 6:20

105

If you are not feeling very well, don't call up all your friends and tell them you are sick. If you keep on doing that, you will end up dead, and they will have to come and bury you.

Norvel Hayes

Death and life are determined by the tongue: the talkative must take the consequences.

Proverbs 18:21
Moffatt

What you do with your eyes in some cases is a matter of life and death. To look at the sickness brings death. To look at God's Word brings life.

Gloria Copeland

And Moses made a bronze serpent and set it on the standard; and it came about, that if a serpent bit any man, when he looked to the bronze serpent, he lived.... And as Moses lifted up the serpent in the wilderness, even so must the Son of Man be lifted up; that whoever believes may in Him have eternal life.

Numbers 21:9; John 3:14,15 NAS

107

God wants you to have long life, for you are needed in the earth more than you are needed in heaven.

Billy Joe Daugherty

Therefore, my brethren, you also were made to die to the Law through the body of Christ, that you might be joined to another, to Him who was raised from the dead, that we might bear fruit for God.

Romans 7:4 NAS

108

Miracles begin within us and then affect our surroundings.

Reinhard Bonnke

I will not venture to speak of anything except what Christ has accomplished through me in leading the Gentiles to obey God by what I have said and done – by the power of signs and miracles, through the power of the Spirit....

Romans 15:18,19 NIV

109

The Lord heals you for His glory and that from henceforth your life shall glorify Him.

Smith Wigglesworth

I shall not die but live, and shall declare the works and recount the illustrious acts of the LORD.

Psalm 118:17 AMP

As long as we live in the thought that we must get sick, though the LORD will heal us, and not rather take dominion over sickness, refusing to tolerate it, it will ever be a menace to us.

Gordon Lindsay

And the LORD shall make you the head, and not the tail; and you shall be above only, and you shall not be beneath, if you heed the commandments of the LORD your God, which I command you this day and are watchful to do them.

Deuteronomy 28:13
AMP

111

Righteousness means the ability to stand in the presence of the Father, or of demons, or of sickness and disease, without the sense of inferiority, condemnation, or of sin-consciousness.

E.W. Kenyon

For God did not give us a spirit of timidity (of cowardice, of craven and cringing and fawning fear), but [He has given us a spirit] of power and of love and of calm and well-balanced mind and discipline and self-control.

2 Timothy 1:7 AMP

Take the shackles off God. Jesus did not heal the sick in order to coax them to be Christians. He healed because it was His nature to heal.

John G. Lake

If ye then, being evil, know how to give good gifts unto your children, how much more shall your Father which is in heaven give good things to them that ask him?

Matthew 7:11

113

Every saint has a blood-bought right to be healed, but thousands do not know that they must exercise the very same appropriating faith in the bruised body of Christ for their healing as they formerly exercised in His shed blood for their salvation.

Dr. T.J. McCrossan

For the life of the flesh is in the blood....

Leviticus 17:11

114

We do not glorify
God in our *spirit*
by remaining in sin.
We do not glorify
God in our *body*
by remaining sick.

T.L. Osborn

*For ye are bought
with a price:
therefore glorify
God in your body,
and in your spirit,
which are God's.*

1 Corinthians 6:20

115

When you begin to rationalize, you find yourself in trouble with the Word of God. You can end up rationalizing away God's promises!

Marilyn Hickey

Trust in the LORD with all your heart, and do not lean on your own understanding. Do not be wise in your own eyes; fear the LORD and turn away from evil. It will be healing to your body, and refreshment to your bones.

Proverbs 3:5,7,8 NAS

We don't deny the existence of the disease; we deny the right of the disease to exist in our bodies.

Jerry Savelle

Know ye not that ye are the temple of God, and that the Spirit of God dwelleth in you?

1 Corinthians 3:16

God is telling you that you are healed; your body is telling you that you are sick. Who are you going to believe? Whichever one that you confess is what you will have.

Frederick K.C. Price

Death and life are in the power of the tongue, and they who indulge in it shall eat the fruit of it [for death or life].

Proverbs 18:21 AMP

118

When faith has a tendency to waver, it is patience that comes to faith's aid to make it stand.

Kenneth Copeland

Knowing this, that the trying of your faith worketh patience.

James 1:3

Faith brings the expectation of the fulfillment of God's promises. Expect God to heal you!

Billy Joe Daugherty

He who did not spare His own Son, but delivered Him up for us all, how will He not also with Him freely give us all things?

Romans 8:32 NAS

Believe you receive in the faith realm, and you shall have it in the natural realm.

John Osteen

And behold, a leper came up to Him and, prostrating himself, worshiped Him, saying, LORD, if You are willing, You are able to cleanse me by curing me. And He reached out His hand and touched him, saying, I am willing; be cleansed by being cured. And instantly his leprosy was cured and cleansed.

Matthew 8:2,3 AMP

To be occupied with symptoms and influenced by them, instead of God's Word, is to question the veracity of God.

F.F. Bosworth

God is not a man, that he should lie, nor a son of man, that he should change his mind. Does he speak and then not act? Does he promise and not fulfill?

Numbers 23:19 NIV

Never show the devil an ounce of weakness. If Satan can detect any kind of weakness in your voice at all, he will whip you.

Norvel Hayes

Put on God's whole armor [the armor of a heavy-armed soldier which God supplies], that you may be able successfully to stand up against [all] the strategies and the deceits of the devil.

Ephesians 6:11 AMP

You won't get anything from God by humoring someone else. You can't ride Momma's coattail into heaven. And you can't ride Momma's coattail into divine healing, either.

Kenneth E. Hagin

I will say of the LORD, He is my refuge and my fortress: my God; in him will I trust.

Psalm 91:2

124

Doctors may have told you there is no hope for you medically, but you can always find supernatural HOPE from God's Word....

Charles Capps

For everything that was written in the past was written to teach us, so that through endurance and the encouragement of the Scriptures we might have hope.

Romans 15:4 NIV

Don't get bitter or
angry at God.
Fight the devil.
God wants you well.

Dodie Osteen

*The thief cometh
not, but for to steal,
and to kill, and to
destroy: I am come
that they might
have life, and that
they might have it
more abundantly.*

John 10:10

The power of faith is the ability to see that which does not exist.

Lester Sumrall

He staggered not at the promise of God through unbelief; but was strong in faith, giving glory to God; and being fully persuaded that, what he had promised, he was able also to perform.

Romans 4:20,21

127

It is wrong for us to have sickness and disease in our bodies when God laid those diseases on Jesus. He became sick with our diseases, that we might be healed.

E.W. Kenyon

Who his own self bare our sins in his own body on the tree, that we, being dead to sins, should live unto righteousness: by whose stripes ye were healed.

1 Peter 2:24

It is the work of the Holy Spirit to keep making life in these mortal bodies of ours.

Dr. T.J. McCrossan

But if the Spirit of him that raised up Jesus from the dead dwell in you, he that raised up Christ from the dead shall also quicken your mortal bodies by his Spirit that dwelleth in you.

Romans 8:11

Faith finds in the Word what belongs to us through the plan of redemption. We take hold with the hand of faith because everything He has is ours. It belongs to us!

Mark Brazee

The Spirit itself beareth witness with our spirit, that we are the children of God: And if children, then heirs; heirs of God, and joint-heirs with Christ; if so be that we suffer with him, that we may be also glorified together.

Romans 8:16,17

It is up to us to get off the pew, and get out into the highways and byways and begin to minister to sick people with authority.

John Osteen

And as ye go, preach, saying, The Kingdom of heaven is at hand. Heal the sick, cleanse the lepers, raise the dead, cast out devils: freely ye have received, freely give.

Matthew 10:7,8

Read the Word. Meditate on the Word. That's taking God's medicine. If you will be faithful to take it continually, it eventually will be as hard for you to get sick as it ever was for you to get well.

Gloria Copeland

My son, attend to my words; consent and submit to my sayings. Let them not depart from your sight; keep them in the center of your heart. For they are life to those who find them, healing and health to all their flesh.

Proverbs 4:20-22
AMP

If you allow your faith to be affected by your senses, you will be defeated in every encounter of life. If, on the other hand, you allow your faith to be governed only by God's Word, you can be nothing less than a winner.

Frederick K.C. Price

Then Jesus told him, "Because you have seen me, you have believed; blessed are those who have not seen and yet have believed."

John 20:29 NIV

God wants to open your blind eyes, deliver you from drugs, heal your suffering body, put your marriage back together and free you from guilt and depression. But He can't release His full miracle-working power through your life until He has your heart.

R.W. Schambach

For the eyes of the LORD run to and fro throughout the whole earth, to shew himself strong in the behalf of them whose heart is perfect toward him.

2 Chronicles 16:9

Christians need never be sick, any more than they need to be sinful. It is always God's desire to heal you.

T.L. Osborn

The Eternal sustains him on a sick bed, and brings him back to health.

Psalm 41:3 Moffatt

The life of sickness, poverty, worry, stress, anxiety and confusion that so many believers live is not the kind of life that Jesus Christ died to provide.

Norvel Hayes

May grace (God's favor) and peace, (which is perfect well-being, all necessary good, all spiritual prosperity, and freedom from fears and agitating passions and moral conflicts) be multiplied to you in [the full, personal, precise and correct] knowledge of God and of Jesus our LORD. For His divine power has bestowed upon us all things that [are requisite and suited] to life and godliness, through the [full, personal] knowledge of Him Who called us by and to His own glory and excellence (virtue).

2 Peter 1:2,3 AMP

...We are completely willing to go to the doctor and get an antibiotic prescription, take it three times a day for ten days, and not even expect to be well until our antibiotics are nearly gone. Why, then, are we too stubborn to press in consistently and persistently with the Word of God for our healing?

Cheryl Salem

For the LORD shall be thy confidence, and shall keep thy foot from being taken.

Proverbs 3:26

When receiving healing by faith, the body and its sensations are lost sight of and only the LORD and His promises are in view.

F.F. Bosworth

So let us seize and hold fast and retain without wavering the hope we cherish and confess and our acknowlegement of it, for He Who promised is reliable (sure) and faithful to His word.

Hebrews 10:23 AMP

Mankind has a right to health, as he has a right to deliverance from sin. If you do not have it, it is because you are being cheated out of your inheritance. It belongs to you. In the name of Jesus Christ, go after it and get it.

John G. Lake

Bless the LORD, O my soul, and forget not all his benefits: Who forgiveth all thine iniquities; who healeth all thy diseases.

Psalm 103:2,3

140

The object of His being made sick with our diseases was that we might be perfectly healed with His life.

E.W. Kenyon

But He was wounded for our transgressions, He was bruised for our guilt and iniquities; the chastisement [needful to obtain] peace and well-being for us was upon Him, and with the stripes [that wounded] Him we are healed and made whole.

Isaiah 53:5 AMP

The Bible pictures Jesus as the *Deliverer* of men and women – *not as their destroyer*.

Kenneth E. Hagin

For the Son of man is not come to destroy men's lives, but to save them....

Luke 9:56

If Jesus – while He was on the earth – wouldn't tolerate any sickness in *His body*, why does He want to tolerate any sickness in *His body* now that He's seated at the right hand of the Majesty on High?

Frederick K.C. Price

And He put all things in subjection under His feet, and gave Him as head over all things to the church, which is His body, the fulness of Him who fills all in all.

Ephesians 1:22,23
NAS

You must believe that you
are healed before you see
the results in your body.
You cannot wait until
your body looks and feels
healed before you believe it.
If you do, you will
never receive by faith.

Kenneth Copeland

Do not, therefore, fling away your fearless confidence, for it carries a great and glorious compensation of reward. For you have need of steadfast patience and endurance, so that you may perform and fully accomplish the will of God, and thus receive and carry away [and enjoy to the full] what is promised.

Hebrews 10:35,36 AMP

This is acting faith: checking health and strength from the Bank of God.

F.F. Bosworth

But they that wait upon the LORD shall renew their strength; they shall mount up with wings as eagles; they shall run, and not be weary; and they shall walk, and not faint.

Isaiah 40:31

146

You have to put the Word of God in your heart until the reality of your healing has more power and more validity to you than the symptoms of sickness that are coming on your body.

Gloria Copeland

My son, attend to my words; incline thine ear unto my sayings. Let them not depart from thine eyes; keep them in the midst of thine heart. For they are life unto those that find them, and health to all their flesh.

Proverbs 4:20-22

Your faith for healing cannot go beyond your knowledge of the Word, for God's Word is the platform from which faith is launched.

Billy Joe Daugherty

How then shall they call on him in whom they have not believed? and how shall they believe in him of whom they have not heard? So then faith cometh by hearing, and hearing by the word of God.

Romans 10:14,17

Divine healing and health is not an optional benefit which we may accept or reject as we see fit, but God made it a statute and an ordinance. He commands us to be well.

Gordon Lindsay

"I call heaven and earth to witness against you today, that I have set before you life and death, the blessing and the curse. So choose life in order that you may live, you and your descendants."

Deuteronomy 30:19
NAS

The prayer of faith has power in it. The prayer of faith has trust in it. The prayer of faith has healing in it for soul and body.

John G. Lake

The prayer of faith will restore the sick man, and the LORD will raise him up; even the sins he has committed will be forgiven him.

James 5:15 Moffatt

The body and the soul have been created to serve together as a habitation of God; the sickly condition of the body is – as well that of the soul – a consequence of sin, and that is what Jesus is come to bear, to expiate and to conquer.

Andrew Murray

But if the Spirit of Him who raised Jesus from the dead dwells in you, He who raised Christ Jesus from the dead will also give life to your mortal bodies through His Spirit who indwells you.

Romans 8:11 NAS

God's *promises* to heal are as much a revelation of His *will* to heal as His *promises* to save are a revelation of His *will* to save.

T.L. Osborn

Then they cry to the Lord in their trouble, and He delivers them out of their distresses. He sends forth His word and heals them and rescues them from the pit and destruction.

Psalm 107:19,20
AMP

This is faith healing – simply believing that you have received the healing because the Word of God says, "That with His stripes ye were (are) healed."

Frederick K.C. Price

For this reason I am telling you, whatever you ask for in prayer, believe (trust and be confident) that it is granted to you, and you will [get it].

Mark 11:24 AMP

153

When you are faced with a life-and-death crisis, the most important thing you can remind yourself of is that God's mercy endures forever.

Creflo Dollar, Jr.

O give thanks unto the LORD; for he is good: for his mercy endureth for ever.

Psalm 136:1

154

The seated Christ is a receipt in full for your healing.

E.W. Kenyon

And what is the exceeding greatness of his power to us-ward who believe, according to the working of his mighty power, which he wrought in Christ, when he raised him from the dead, and set him at his own right hand in the heavenly places, far above all principality, and power, and might, and dominion, and every name that is named, not only in this world, but also in that which is to come.

Ephesians 1:19-21

Not only is it God's will to heal, it is God's will to heal all!

Jerry Savelle

How God anointed and consecrated Jesus of Nazareth with the [Holy] Spirit and with strength and ability and power; how He went about doing good and, in particular, curing all who were harassed and oppressed by [the power of] the devil, for God was with Him.

Acts 10:38 AMP

References

Prayer For Healing

Father, Your Word says that whatever I ask for in prayer, if I believe I've received it, it will be mine. So I come to Your throne boldly by faith to receive healing of _____.

Thank You that Jesus took my sicknesses, carried away my diseases, and provided healing for me 2,000 years ago. Healing isn't something You might do, or could do, or would do if I were good enough; healing is something that You've already done for me. Because of the stripes on Jesus' back, I believe that I am healed now. Sickness is under the curse of the law, and Jesus saved me from the curse; so that means that Jesus saved me from this sickness.

Because You are the God Who heals me, I refuse to let this sickness stay in my body. I won't tolerate it. Satan has to take his hands off me because I am God's property. I have on the whole armor of God, and the shield of faith protects me from all the fiery darts of the devil.

Healing is the children's bread and I'm Your child; so I receive total and complete healing for my body and mind, from the top of my head to the soles of my feet. You've given me Your Word on it, and that's good enough for me.

I believe that I'm beginning to get better right now, from this very moment. I may or may not feel better right away, but my faith is not based on what I feel, or what I see; it's based on Jesus, the Word of God. If Jesus said it, I believe it. His Word never lies.

Father, Your Word says that my tongue has the power of life and death, so please help me to speak over my body only words filled with faith, hope, life and health. I will not let any words of sickness, death or unbelief cross my lips.

Because faith calls those things that be not as though they were, I call myself healed. Father, thank You for healing me.

In Jesus' name I pray. Amen.

Scripture References

Isaiah 53:5   Matthew 18:18   Galatians 3:13   Mark 1:23, 24
1 Peter 2:24   Mark 16:17, 18   Psalm 103:3   John 14:14
1 John 3:8   Psalm 91:2   John 10:10   Proverbs 4:20-22
Luke 10:19   Proverbs 18:21

The Harrison House Vision

Proclaiming the truth and the power
Of the Gospel of Jesus Christ
With excellence;

Challenging Christians to
Live victoriously,
Grow spiritually,
Know God intimately.

Additional copies of this book are available
from your local bookstore.

Harrison House
P. O. Box 35035
Tulsa, Oklahoma 74153